For the Love of
ROTTWEILERS

For the Love of
ROTTWEILERS

Robert Hutchinson

BrownTrout Publishers
San Francisco

Rottweilers Photography Credits

Cover		©1998
p.2/3		©1998 Mark Raycroft
4/5		©1998 Zandria Muench Beraldo
6		©1998 Mark Raycroft
7		©1998 Zandria Muench Beraldo
8/9		©1998 Zandria Muench Beraldo
10/11		©1998 Mark Raycroft
12/13		©1998 J.W. Stetzholz
14/15		©1998 Mark Raycroft
16		©1998 Zandria Muench Beraldo
17	(top)	©1998 Mark Raycroft
17	(bottom)	©1998 Mark Raycroft
18/19		©1998 Zandria Muench Beraldo
20/21		©1998 Mark Raycroft
22/23		©1998 Zandria Muench Beraldo
24		©1998 Mark Raycroft
25		©1998 Mark Raycroft
26/27		©1998 Sharon Eide & Elizabeth Flynn
28/29		©1998 Sharon Eide & Elizabeth Flynn
30/31		©1998 Kent & Donna Dannen
32		©1998 Mark Raycroft
33	(top)	©1998 Sharon Eide & Elizabeth Flynn
33	(bottom)	©1998 Zandria Muench Beraldo
34		©1998 Jerry Shulman
35		©1998 Sharon Eide & Elizabeth Flynn
36/37		©1998 Mark Raycroft
38		©1998 Mark Raycroft
39		©1998 J.W. Stetzholz
40/41		©1998 J.W. Stetzholz
42		©1998 Sharon Eide & Elizabeth Flynn
43	(top)	©1998 Zandria Muench Beraldo
43	(bottom)	©1998 Sharon Eide & Elizabeth Flynn
44/45		©1998 Mark Raycroft
46/47		©1998 Zandria Muench Beraldo
48		©1998 Mark Raycroft
49	(top)	©1998 Mark Raycroft
49	(bottom)	©1998 Jerry Shulman
50/51		©1998 Zandria Muench Beraldo
52/53		©1998 Mark Raycroft
54/55		©1998 Mark Raycroft
56		©1998 Sharon Eide & Elizabeth Flynn
57		©1998 Zandria Muench Beraldo
58/59		©1998 Alan & Sandy Carey
60/61		©1998 Sharon Eide & Elizabeth Flynn
62/63		©1998 Zandria Muench Beraldo
64/65		©1998 Sharon Eide & Elizabeth Flynn
66		©1998 Mark Raycroft
67	(top)	©1998 Zandria Muench Beraldo
67	(bottom)	©1998 Mark Raycroft
68/69		©1998 Zandria Muench Beraldo
70/71		©1998 Mark Raycroft
72/73		©1998 Zandria Muench Beraldo
74		©1998 Mark Raycroft
75	(top)	©1998 Zandria Muench Beraldo
75	(bottom)	©1998 Mark Raycroft
76/77		©1998 Zandria Muench Beraldo
78/79		©1998 Zandria Muench Beraldo
80/81		©1998 J.W. Stetzholz
81		©1998 Kent & Donna Dannen
82		©1998 Mark Raycroft
83		©1998 Mark Raycroft
84/85		©1998 W. Holzworth
86		©1998 Mark Raycroft
87		©1998 Mark Raycroft
88/89		©1998 Mark Raycroft
90		©1998 Sharon Eide & Elizabeth Flynn
91	(top)	©1998 Mark Raycroft
91	(bottom)	©1998 Mark Raycroft
92/93		©1998 Mark Raycroft
94/95		©1998 Mark Raycroft
96/97		©1998 Sharon Eide & Elizabeth Flynn
98/99		©1998 Zandria Muench Beraldo
100		©1998 Sharon Eide & Elizabeth Flynn
101	(top)	©1998 Zandria Muench Beraldo
101	(bottom)	©1998 J.W. Stetzholz
102/103		©1998 Mark Raycroft
104/105		©1998 Mark Raycroft
106/107		©1998 Zandria Muench Beraldo
108		©1998 Mark Raycroft
109	(top)	©1998 J.W. Stetzholz
109	(bottom)	©1998 Zandria Muench Beraldo
110/111		©1998 Zandria Muench Beraldo

Library of Congress Cataloging-in-Publication Data
Rottweilers / Robert Hutchinson
     p.   cm. — (For the love of—)
    ISBN 1-56313-900-6 (alk. paper)
    1. Rottweiler dog.   I. Title.   II. Series:
Hutchinson, Robert, 1951–   For the love of—
[SF429.R7H87   1998]
636.73—dc21
                                           98-41253
                                        CIP

Printed and bound in Italy by Milanostampa

ISBN: 1-56313-900-6 (alk. paper)
10 9 8 7 6 5 4 3 2 1
Digit on the right indicates the number of this printing

Published by:
BrownTrout Publishers, Inc.
Post Office Box 280070
San Francisco, California 94128-0070 U.S.A.

Toll Free: 800 777 7812
Website: browntrout.com

Charisma of the Rottweiler

Our camera tracks across the show-room toward the awesome machine on the dais. Its backlit silhouette is a bold composition of clean orthogonal lines and crisp arcs. Though stationary, the compact form seems to ripple with coiled energy. Our camera swings into a low-angle 360. A broad, angulated front-end suspended elastically on sturdy vertical columns… topline and underline running straight, parallel, true… rear-end assembly a sleek longitudinal alignment of propulsive curves. Uncompromising engineering. Consummate design. A masterpiece. A Rottweiler.

The Rottweiler breed represents one of the triumphs of twentieth-century German engineering. Like the BMW, the Rottweiler was developed by rigorously applying static and kinetic mechanics to systems design in order to optimize strength, power, and handling. Unlike the BMW, the Rottweiler is the product of genetic engineering.

To be sure, all the lesser dog breeds of the world are equally creatures of genetic engineering. Hey, no breeder: no breed. Left to themselves, dogs cheerfully flout all breed distinctions and array themselves in continuous variation around a mongrel mean. Only human curbs to canine wanton-ness can segregate dogs into breeds. Yet, once isolated in the Petrie dish of a breeding program, the germ plasm of *Canis familiaris* yields with almost magical plasticity to the most preposterous exaggerations conceived by human whim. As a consequence, breed diversity in the dog far exceeds that in any

other domesticated species. A succession of like-minded breeders can shrink a dog to the size of a rat; bury it under masses of hair; or tumble its skin into concertina folds.

What makes the Rottweiler a triumph of genetic engineering is not some fanciful distortion of a single feature. The distinction of the Rottweiler inheres in the subtle poetry of its overall systems design, which strives toward a beautiful proportion and balance among all of its traits — behavioral as much as physical. Excellence in design and execution never goes unappreciated in the United States. Three decades ago, the Rottweiler was an exotic curiosity in this country. Today, with 75,489 AKC registrations in 1997, the Rottweiler ranks as our most popular working breed and the second most popular breed overall.

The equipoise of its parts that distinguishes the Rottweiler breed has been crafted by a brilliant program of artificial selection that began at the turn of this century in southwest Germany and that continues to this day to be scrupulously maintained and fine-tuned by dedicated Rottweiler breeders throughout the world. What can be told from surviving records of the birth and early development of this program in Germany follows.

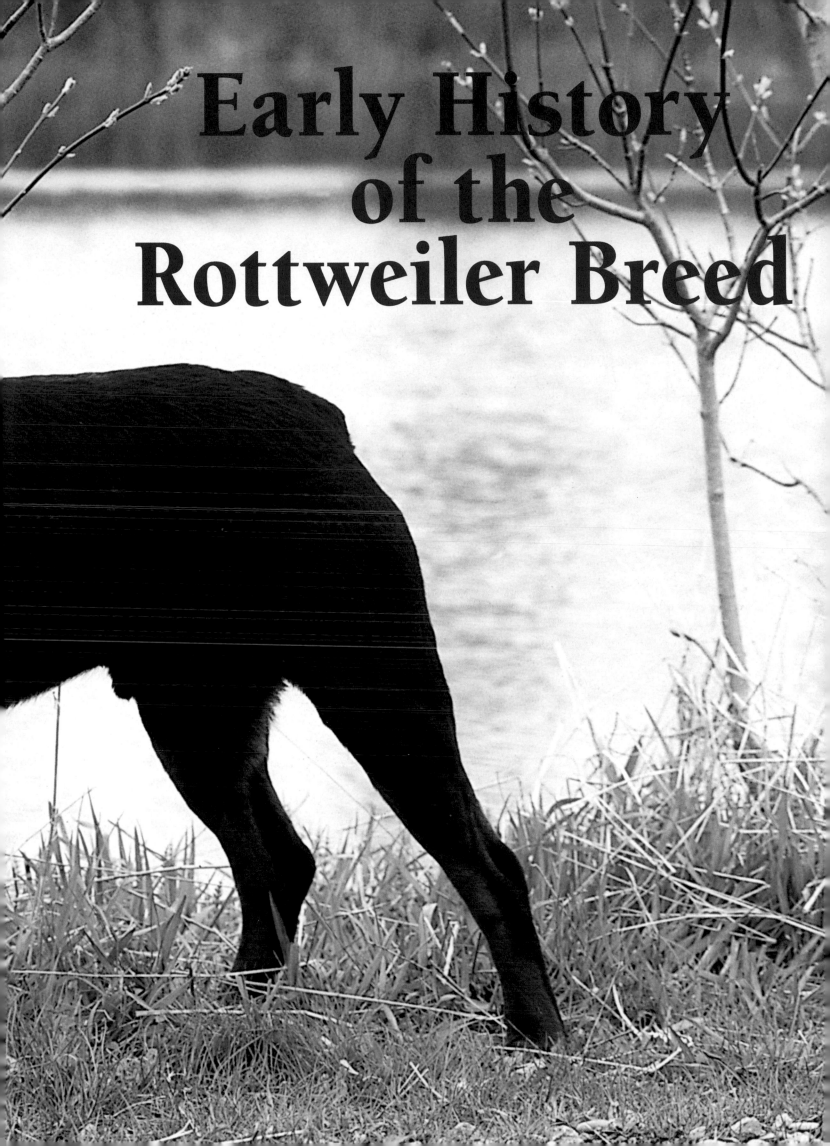

Early History of the Rottweiler Breed

Breeds, in the proper sense of the word, are the products of comprehensive artificial selection within the framework of systematic breeding programs. Every trait matters. Breeders take pains to select for as many as possible of the global set of traits, each minutely prescribed in a breed protocol. A breed is the sum of many exact intentions, each realized by pinpoint genetic manipulation.

Systematic breeding programs, whether for dogs or livestock, are predicated on the efficient cooperation of two regulatory mechanisms: shows and breed societies. Shows judge animals in both objective trials against formal standards and competitive trials against other animals. Breed societies authorize judges, shows, breed standards, and

local breed clubs; register suitable animals; and record show results. Shows and societies work in tandem to establish, preserve, and improve a breed by ensuring that those animals selected for mating will in fact be the most suitable.

The dog is the oldest domesticated animal. Since the days of the Pharaohs, specialty dogs have been unsystematically bred in the kennels of the ruling classes. Genetic integrity in the historical dog "breeds" was confined to local strains as an accident of the *de facto* line breeding that resulted when self-perpetuating dog packs were sequestered in manorial kennels. Even in such special closed environments, however, systematic breeding was impossible in the absence of thorough record keeping or of genetic methodology. Systematic breeding of livestock was begun in the eighteenth century by Bakewell of Dishley. Because of its freedom of intercourse and low economic value, the dog was not subjected to systematic breeding until the nineteenth century. The first dog show was held in 1859 in Newcastle-upon-Tyne, England. The first dog breed society, the Kennel Club of England, was formed in 1873.

The first dog show in Germany, held in Hamburg in 1863, had an entry of 543 dogs — none called *Rottweiler.* The first recorded use of the term *Rottweiler* in connection with a dog is a reference to a single dog entered in that category in a dog show in Heilbronn (in the lower Neckar Valley, Kingdom of Württemberg, German Empire) in 1882. O. Hell wrote in 1926, the year that he assumed leadership of Germany's national Rottweiler breed society, that the dog denominated *Rottweiler* in the 1882 show "bore little resemblance to our present requirements" — being nearly the same height but only half the weight of its modern namesake.

The second recorded use of the term *Rottweiler* occurs in the caption to a studio photograph, dated 1890, in which a dog is shown double-harnessed with an old peasant woman to a cart. All the features of this dog mark it as a common herding-dog type: long legs; narrow trunk; thin bone; flat musculature; shallow forechest; flat skull; long, narrow muzzle; large ears; steeply sloping croup; extensive markings on the chest and white socks. Apart from its dark ground color, the only point of resemblance with our modern Rottweiler breed is a certain squarishness of build implicit in the vertically straight lower leg and horizontally straight lumbar segment of the topline.

Apart from these two spectral appearances, the *Rottweiler* counts as a complete cipher in the booming dog-breed world of late nineteenth century Germany. In 1887, King Karl of Württemberg sponsored a show in Stuttgart (also in the Neckar Valley, just fifty miles downriver of the town of Rottweil) with an entry of 660 dogs — none a *Rottweiler.* In 1888, the first enduring German dog breed society, the *Deutsche Dogge Klub* (Great Dane Club), was founded in Frankfurt. Sixteen more German dog breed societies followed in the next decade, each with its own breed book. In addition, a national all-breed stud book (*Das Deutsche Hundestammbuch*, **DHStB**) and all-breed working-dog stud book (*Das Deutsche Gebrauchshundestammbuch*, **DGStB**) were opened — neither listing any *Rottweiler.* In 1894, Ludwig Beckmann published his definitive study of dog breeds, *Die Rassen des Hundes* (The Breeds

of Dog) — containing no mention of *Rottweiler*.

When the *Rottweiler* did eventually receive the recognition of a breed society, the manifestation was again spectral. The third recorded use of the term *Rottweiler* occurs in 1899, when a shadowy figure named Albert Kull founded a breed society called the *Internationale Klub für Leonberger und Rottweiler Hunde* (IKLRH, International Club for Leonberger and Rottweiler Dogs). The Leonberger is a tawny-coated giant breed introduced in 1846 by an alderman of Leonberg, a little town near Stuttgart, who had expressly developed the dog to imitate the eponymous lion in his town's coat-of-arms. By cross-breeding Saint Bernard with Landseer Newfoundland, the alderman contrived such a leonine effect that, beginning in 1870, royalty throughout Europe adopted the fashion of decorating their courts with these living heraldic devices. By the last decade of the century, the Czar's court alone was importing three hundred Leonbergers annually. In 1895, the *Internationale Klub für Leonberger Hunde* (IKLH: International Club for Leonberger Dogs) was founded in Stuttgart to impose quality controls on the burgeoning and profitable breed.

Kull's new club (differing in name from its predecessor only by the insertion of *und Rottweiler*) was a flop. Its very existence would be unknown if not for the discovery in the mid-1960's of some disjointed documents in the estate of a dead cynologist. One of the documents was the *Rassekennzeichen des Internationalen Klub für Leonberger und Rottweiler Hunde* (Breed Standard of the IKLRH), ostensibly written by Kull in 1883 but not adopted by his Club until 1901. Curiously, this document nowhere declares that it applies to one rather than the other of the club's

two titular breeds. Except for the coat, all the points in Kull's standard are described in such a non-quantitative and non-restrictive way that they might apply with equal propriety to both the Leonberger and the Rottweiler as represented in their respective modern breed standards. With respect to coat, the IKLRH Standard states it must be "long... and very abundant" and that its color should be "preferably and most commonly black with russet or yellow markings... Alternatively black stripes on an ash-gray background with yellow markings; plain red...; dark wolf-gray with black head and saddle..." The modern breed standards specify that the Leonberger coat must be "abundantly long" and in the gamut between red and pale-yellow; and that the Rottweiler coat must be of medium length and black-and-tan. The IKLRH Breed Standard seems to describe a Leonberger with dark hair.

The fourth and fifth recorded references to *Rottweiler* both come in 1905 — the breakthrough year for the breed. In this year, the Rottweiler breed received its first published mention. In his book, *Die Deutschen Hunde und Ihre Abstammung* (German Dogs and Their Descent), Richard Strebel included both a drawing of a *Rottweiler* dog and an account of the breed's origin. The drawing depicts a dog that adumbrates our modern Rottweiler in some forequarter features: squarish build (with length-to-height ratio of 1.15); capacious chest; moderately deep muzzle. Most of the points of its conformation, however, are at variance with the compact, robust *Gestalt* of our modern Rottweiler. The Rottweiler in Strebel's drawing more closely resembles the Rottweiler in the 1890 photograph insofar as it is lanky in the legs; thin in the bone; light in musculature; tucked up in the

loin; subdued in the stop; narrow in the forehead; long in the muzzle; and extensively marked. Strebel's text asserts that the Rottweiler originated as a specialty breed imported from Ancient Rome to do double-duty as a droving-dog and war-mastiff for the legions stationed at the colony that stood on the site of Rottweil from 74 AD to 260 AD. (The proposition that a dog breed could be preserved intact across four hundred dog generations and a succession of peasant economies in which culling for working ability operated as the only selective technique is scientifically grotesque. Strebel's cross-species inversion of the Romulus and Remus foundation myth has been uncritically retailed as established history in all but a few of the books since written on Rottweilers. Sir Philip Sydney's jibe

that historians authorize themselves "for the most part upon other histories" has never been more telling.)

The other event in 1905 of great moment to the Rottweiler breed was its second recognition in a show. As at the 1882 show, the recognition was accorded to a single dog. This time, however, it was staged with fanfare. At the 1905 Dog Show of the Association of the Friends of Dogs in Heidelberg, the Chairman of the Heidelberg Kennel Club, Karl Knauf, and Albert Graf portentously announced that they would undertake a search for "a fine dog of unusual breed and irreproachable character" to present to the Honorary President of the show. After diligent search, they unveiled their mystery dog: a *Rottweiler*. Graf seized the occasion to declare his intention of

beginning the systematic development of this "unusual breed" by assembling a foundation stock in Heidelberg.

Graf had apparently given himself a head start, for the very next year, 1906, his Rottweiler dog, Russ vom Brückenbuckel, swept first place in Open Class at three International Shows in Worms, Frankfurt, and Darmstadt. In January of 1907, Graf and Knauf founded the first viable Rottweiler breed society, the *Deutsche Rottweiler-Klub* (**DRK**, German Rottweiler Club), in Heidelberg. The first entry in the first volume of the DRK *Zuchtbuchfuhrung* (Breed Book), kept by Secretary Graf, was his own dog, **Russ vom Brückenbuckel** 1 DRZ. Russ's unregistered parents were Flora and Stumper von Heiligenberg. Later in

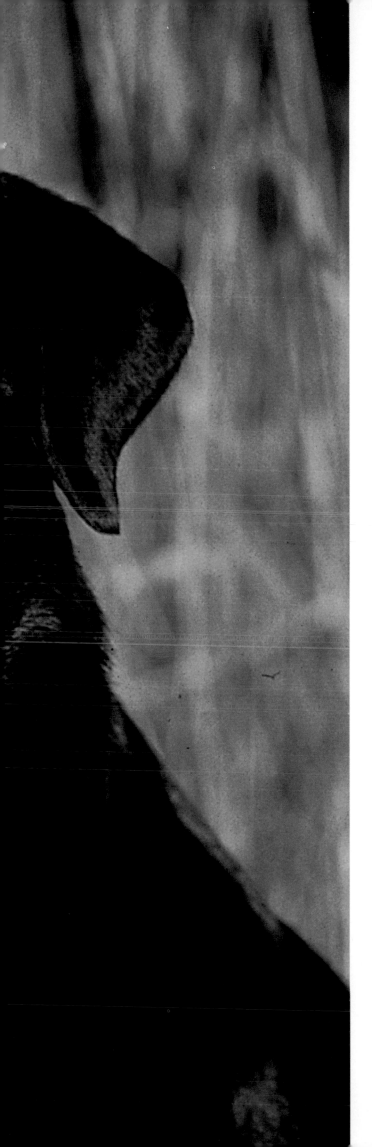

1907, Russ won first prizes in Championship Class at the International Shows in Frankfurt and Mannheim. Sieger **Russ vom Brückenbuckel 1 DRZ** went on to figure as the most prolific stud of DRK's early years, siring a fifth of the 399 dogs in Volume 1 of the DRK Breed Book, which covered the years 1907–1914.

The second dog entered in the DRK Breed Book in 1907 was Sieger **Ralph vom Neckar 2 DKZ**, who would sire a tenth of the dogs in Volume I. Although less prolific than Russ, Ralph produced better progeny. Ralph as he appears in a surviving photograph bears so close a resemblance to the dog in Strebel's 1905 drawing that he might have been its model.

The third most important DRK foundation stud was **Max von der Stahlenberg 48 DRZ**, registered in 1908. In 1909, Max and the adjacent entry, **Flock von Hamburg 49 DRZ**, became the first Rottweiler police dogs. One of their promoters on the Hamburg force, Inspector Hinsch, was rewarded with the leadership of the DRK for having persuaded the *Erste Deutsche Polizeihund Verein* (First German Police Dog Association) in 1910 to recognize the Rottweiler as an official Police Dog Breed (along with the German Shepherd Dog, the Dobermann Pinscher, and the Airedale Terrier). In 1911, DRK Rottweilers began to be exported for use by foreign police. Although all the Rottweiler champions and police dogs of the initial years of the breed were out of the DRK Breed Book, DRK was not the only game in town.

In April 1907, a few months after its founding, DRK expelled an unnamed member for an unspecified "gross infringement." Over the issue, a breakaway group set up a rival breed society, the *Süddeutsche Rottweiler-Klub* (SRK, South German

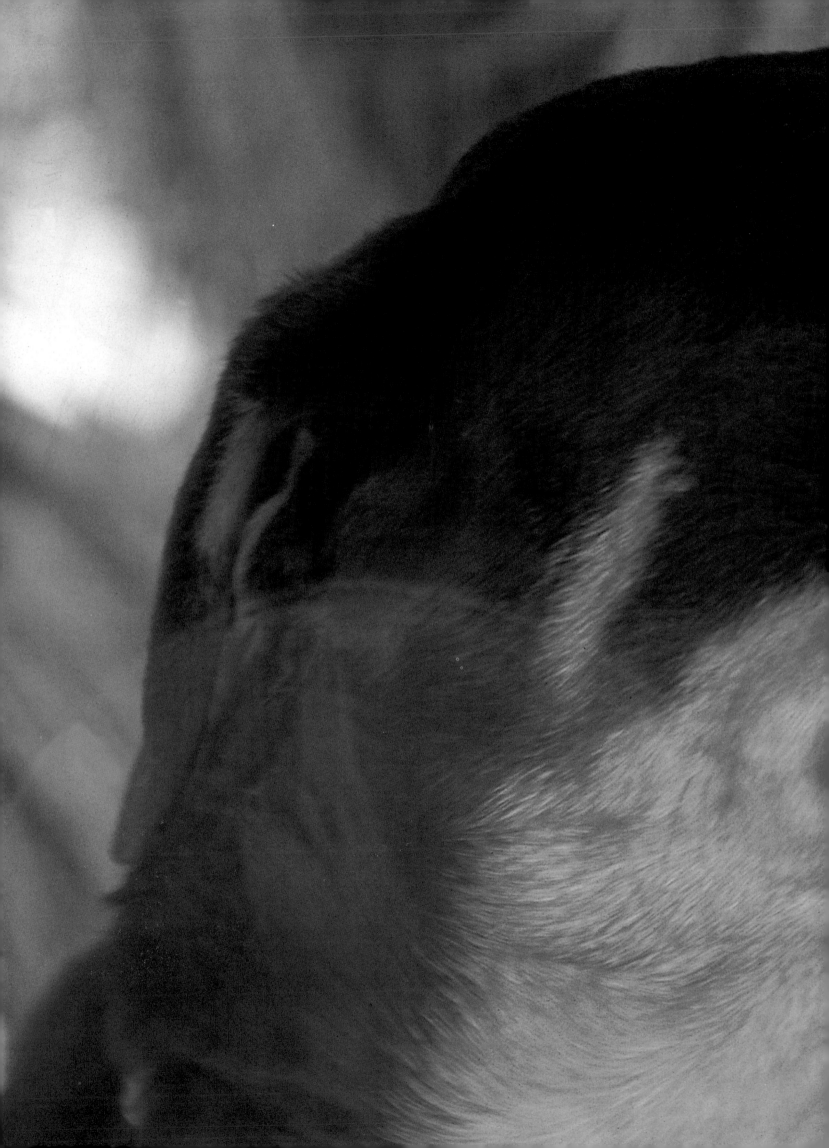

Rottweiler Club). SRK soon changed its name to the *Internationale Rott-weiler-Klub* (**IRK**, International Rottweiler Club). IRK, headquartered like its DRK rival in Heidelberg, began its own Breed Book in 1907. The dynastic fountainhead of IRK was **Leo von Cannstatt** 29 IRZ. Leo was born in July 1908 of unregistered parents, Leo and Fanny von Plattenhardt, bred by Gottlieb Haus of Fildern. Although only 28 of his progeny were entered in the IRK Breed Book, they were to account for all the enduring IRK bloodlines.

Leo's appearance in a surviving photograph contrasts strongly to that of the DRK foundation stock. In body, Leo is much more heavily and broadly built: deeper and broader of chest; stouter in the forelegs; deeper in the loin. The contrast in the head

is even stronger: his muzzle is shorter and deeper; his skull is broader and more domed; his stop is more pronounced; his ears are smaller and higher. In short, Leo's conformation was much more mastiff-like than that of his DRK counterparts.

The most illustrious of Leo's bloodlines ran through his grandson, **Lord Remo von Schifferstadt** 130 IRZ (born 1911), even though Lord Remo exceeded by several inches the maximum height permitted by the IRK Breed Standard. Lord Remo's greatest son, **Sieger Lord von der Teck** 413 IRZ (born 1914), was inbred to his own full sister, **Minna von der Teck** 411 IRZ, to whelp **Sieger Arco Torfwerk** 955 IRZ (born 1918). Arco sired over 100 litters, from which was descended a large proportion of the future champions of the breed, right up to the present.

IRK's efforts to have its dogs recruited for police work were spearheaded by Commissioner Ackernacht of the Frankfurt police force, who headed the IRK from 1912 to 1915. Ackernacht engaged the DRK in merger negotiations in 1913, but club differences over conformation values and appropriate breedstock proved irreconcilable. IRK bloodlines, embodying predominantly mastiff-like features, remained hermetically closed to DRK stock. DRK bloodlines, embodying predominantly hound-like features, had already been opened to limited but conspicuous penetration by descendants of **Leo von Cannstatt** 29 IRZ. One of the arguments in favor of DRK/IRK amalgamation during the 1913 negotiations was the signal success that year, both as show dog and police dog, of **Rhino von Kork** 188 DRZ — son of DRK-founder Russ but grandson of IRK-founder Leo.

At the time of the abortive merger talks, the DRK and IRK Breed Books were neck-and-neck,

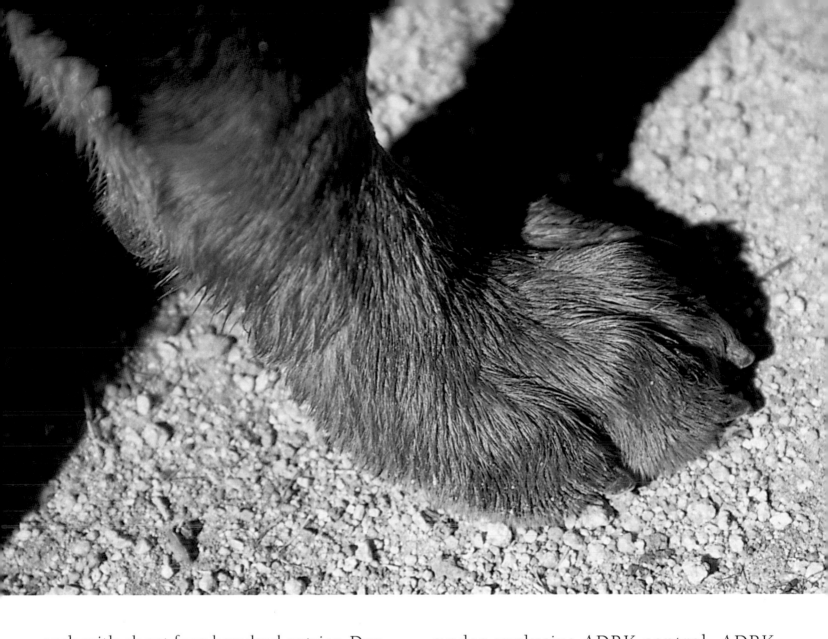

each with about four hundred entries. During the next eight years, however, entries to the IRK Breed Book outstripped the DRK by a factor of four. In 1921, facing extinction by marginalization, DRK capitulated and was absorbed by IRK, which was re-named *Allgemeiner Deutscher Rottweiler-Klub* (**ADRK**, General German Rottweiler Club). ADRK initially incorporated the DRK and IRK Breed Books (as well as the pertinent section of the DHStB) as ongoing independent publications. When the superseding ADRK Breed Book was opened in 1924, however, it was a numerical and genealogical continuation of the IRK Breed Book. ADRK policy and practice over the next few years effectively eliminated DRK stock from the breed.

Our modern Rottweiler has evolved under exclusive ADRK control. ADRK, which remains the sole Rottweiler breed society in its country of origin, has provided the world not only the universal Rottweiler Breed Standard of the *Fédération Cynologique Internationale* but, ultimately, all foreign Rottweiler foundation stock. Every living Rottweiler in the world is, therefore, descended from **Leo von Cannstatt** 29 IRZ.

Genetic Considerations

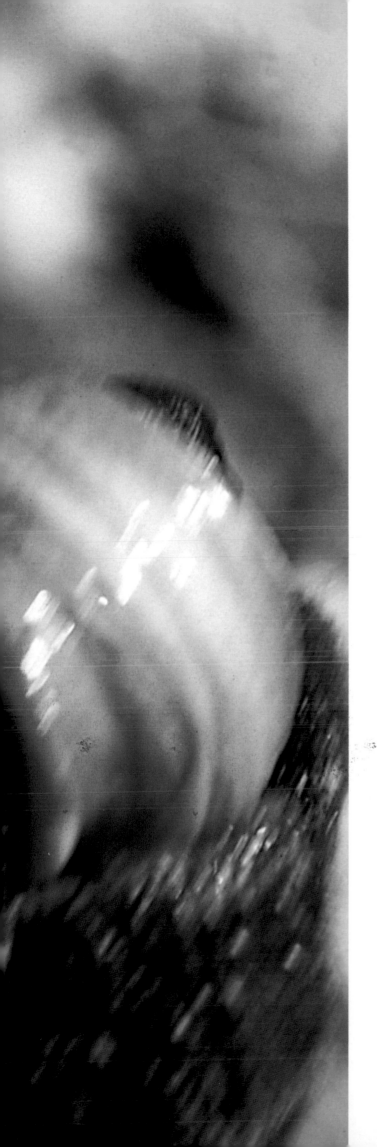

The preceding chronological précis of the scattered documents that have survived from the formative stage of the Rottweiler breed does not constitute a coherent story. Conspicuously missing from the record is any explanation for the two radical transformations in the appearance of the successive dogs called *Rottweiler*. In the first transformation, sometime between 1890 and 1905, the traditional *Rottweiler* morphed from a light and leggy herding-dog type into the markedly heavier dog depicted by Strebel and bred by Graf. Then, sometime before 1908, the proprietary right of the Strebel/Graf/DRK dog to the title of *Rottweiler* was challenged by an unprecedented IRK dog displaying markedly more mastiff-like features. Before we hazard our attempt to link the surviving fragments into a plausible story of the development of the Rottweiler breed from the traditional Rottweiler type, we must chew a bit on the question of the genetic basis of the distinction between dog *type* and dog *breed* and what it takes to get from one to the other.

Dog *types* are at root just job categories. A herding-dog, fighting-dog, or guard-dog *type* is a genetically promiscuous medley of dogs, each happening to possess that minimal subset of traits needed to qualify it to be trained for the job at hand. All the rest of a candidate's traits are irrelevant. As a functional category, guard dog is of a kind with football guard. In both instances, what matters is that the individual be big, strong, and aggressive; whether he have hairless eyelids, undescended testicles, or appalling manners matters not.

A very practical difference exists, however, between an historical working-dog type and a human job category. When an incompetent

human employee gets the ax, he can try another line or go on the dole. An incompetent herding dog in a peasant economy, by contrast, gets the ax quite literally. The herding dog that cannot be absolutely trusted to manage its herd correctly in every situation poses an unacceptable economic hazard to the herdsman. Neither can unemployed dogs be permitted to loaf about in an environment where they will harass and attack livestock. For the less than perfectly competent herding dog, there can be no reprieve in a peasant economy. *Culling* — the practice of eliminating unfit animals — is the form of selection universally practiced on dogs in peasant economies.

The economy of Württemberg was principally agricultural, and the

part of the Kingdom that was most productive of crops and livestock was the Neckar Valley. From time immemorial through the end of the nineteenth century, agriculture in the Neckar Valley was organized as a small-scale, peasant economy. In the absence of manorial estates with kennels for specialty dogs, culling was the only form of artificial selection practiced on dogs in the Neckar Valley until the civic-minded experiments of the alderman of Leonberg. The dogs of the Neckar Valley were strictly workers — no bums, no dandies. In appearance, the dogs of the Neckar were the usual herding-dog motley: miscellaneous colors and features, but all of them leggy and long-muzzled. Behaviorally and temperamentally, they were much more homogeneous: agile, biddable, and dominant toward larger animals. What do such dogs look like genetically?

Compared to a purebred dog, any individual working-type dog is a non-descript slob scrambled up by genetic roulette. Only when viewed as a sort of populational meta-dog does a working-dog type resolve into a more determinate entity, showing a genetic profile tighter than that of a truly random mongrel population. The genetic distinctiveness of a working-dog type is imparted by the slightly heritable effect of culling on the frequency of favored nonadditive traits. Excuse me?

Okay. Even though culling by itself can never develop a breed, it can still foster certain heritable traits in a population. Dogs in a population subject to pervasive culling will be more likely to survive to reproductive maturity if they possess those useful traits that the cullers value. To the extent that those selected traits are heritable, their frequency in the culled population will increase. The rub is that behavioral traits show notoriously low

heritability. Behavioral traits show such low heritability because they are *polygenic* — that is, they depend on combinations of genes at several gene-sites (*loci*). As combinatorial possibilities increase, indeterminacy increases, and heritability decreases. As a result, the distinctiveness of the genetic profile of a working-dog type population is subdued (of low heritability) and cryptic (restricted to polygenic traits).

Opposed to polygenic (or *non-additive*) traits are *simple* (or *additive*) traits that depend on just one pair of genes at one locus. Which of a small set of gene-variants (*alleles*) make up that one pair of genes completely determines the simple trait. Because the possible combinations of these alleles are

few, simple traits show high heritability.

A breeding program is most effective when it focuses on simple traits. The breeder selects for the desirable allele of a simple trait by suitable mating, and selects against the undesirable allele by culling the progeny (non-lethally, nowadays). The frequency of the desirable allele in the breed line increases; the frequency of undesirable allele decreases. As the alleles approach homogeneity (*homozygosity*), the simple trait becomes *fixed* in the breed. Then the breeder can focus on the next simple trait, fix it, and just *add* it to the first.

An example of a simple trait in dogs is coat-length. The Rottweiler breed of today is homozygous for short coat. As a result, heritability of short coat is unity: all Rottweiler progeny are short-coated, too. We know that long coat was very common in the early days of the breed. How long did it take to select out the long coat?

Just to get an idea of scale, suppose that one in every four dogs in the early population was long-coated and that the population was reproductively closed. If all the long-coats were excluded from mating, then (by Falconer's formula) it would take three-and-half generations, or fifteen years, to reach the point that one in every thirty dogs was long-coated.

Stabilization of polygenic traits, because they are much less heritable, is an order of magnitude more time-consuming than for simple traits. Polygenic traits include not only behavioral traits, but also most conformation traits, such as head structure and bone thickness.

Our point can now be made. Fifteen years is hardly enough time to begin to stabilize the high heterozygosity of the simple traits of the 1890 Rottweiler herding-dog type. Fifteen years is not

enough time by an order of magnitude to get from the polygenic conformation features of the 1890 Rottweiler to those of the Strebel/Graf/DRK Rottweiler of 1905 by selection within a closed population. Much less can selection alone go from the DRK to the IRK Rottweiler in three years. Conclusion: the early Rottweiler stock was not a reproductively closed population.

Fortified by this conclusion, we undertake to link the fragmentary early records into a plausible story of the origin of the Rottweiler.

Origin of the Rottweiler Breed

As early as 1883, Kull interested himself in the breeding prospects of the Leonberger in association with those of the Rottweiler. The Rottweiler of this time was an obscure, non-descript, herding-dog type employed in a peasant economy. The Leonberger, by contrast, was a famous, precise *Luxushund* breed calculated to appeal to a cosmetic niche market. When Kull founded IKLRH in 1899, IKLH had already been flourishing for four years. What was Kull's angle in challenging the jurisdiction of an established breed society and in exalting an obscure dog-type to equal rank with a famous dog-breed?

Color-control problems stemming from the Leonberger's cross-bred origin long dogged Leonberger breeders. Even today, after 150 years of intensive selection for tawny colors, rogue colors — black; black-and-tan; brown; silver; taupe — pop up in the breed. A century ago, the colors of Leonberger litters were all over the place. Yet only tawny yellow was salable as *Leonberger*. Did Kull smell a way to rehabilitate the losers in the Leonberger color game?

Kull seems to have conceived a strategy to piggy-back onto the commercially hot Leonberger a new breed — really an anti-breed — that could absorb all those perfectly sound Leonbergers that were disqualified from sale or stud service for lacking the pigmentation of African cats. A purebred Leonberger with a dark coat fetched nothing on the international market. Neither, certainly, did the traditional Rottweiler herding-dog type. But suppose a breeder were to cross individually outstanding Rottweiler herding

dogs with highbred dark Leonbergers. Might he not hope to generate a salable dog possessing many of the commercially proven highbred qualities of the Leonberger but under the more permissive rubric of *Rottweiler*?

Rottweiler, after all, was a great name just looking for the right dog. First, Rottweil was a quaint Swabian town in the Neckar Valley just like Leonberg: no surprise that their dogs should look similar. Second, an antecedent association between the name and a traditional dog-type existed but it was so obscure and ill-defined as to be an open category. The name even has a catchy semantic resonance in German: *Rotte* means "dog pack."

If Kull hoped to redeem the value of imperfect Leonbergers by

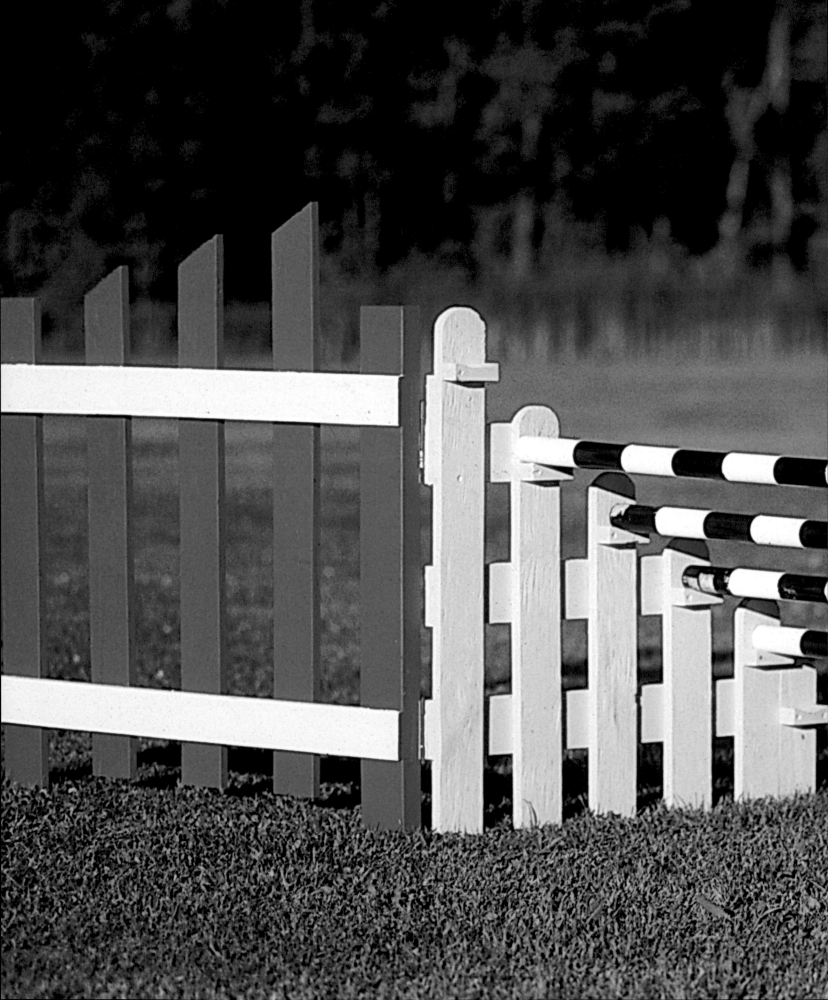

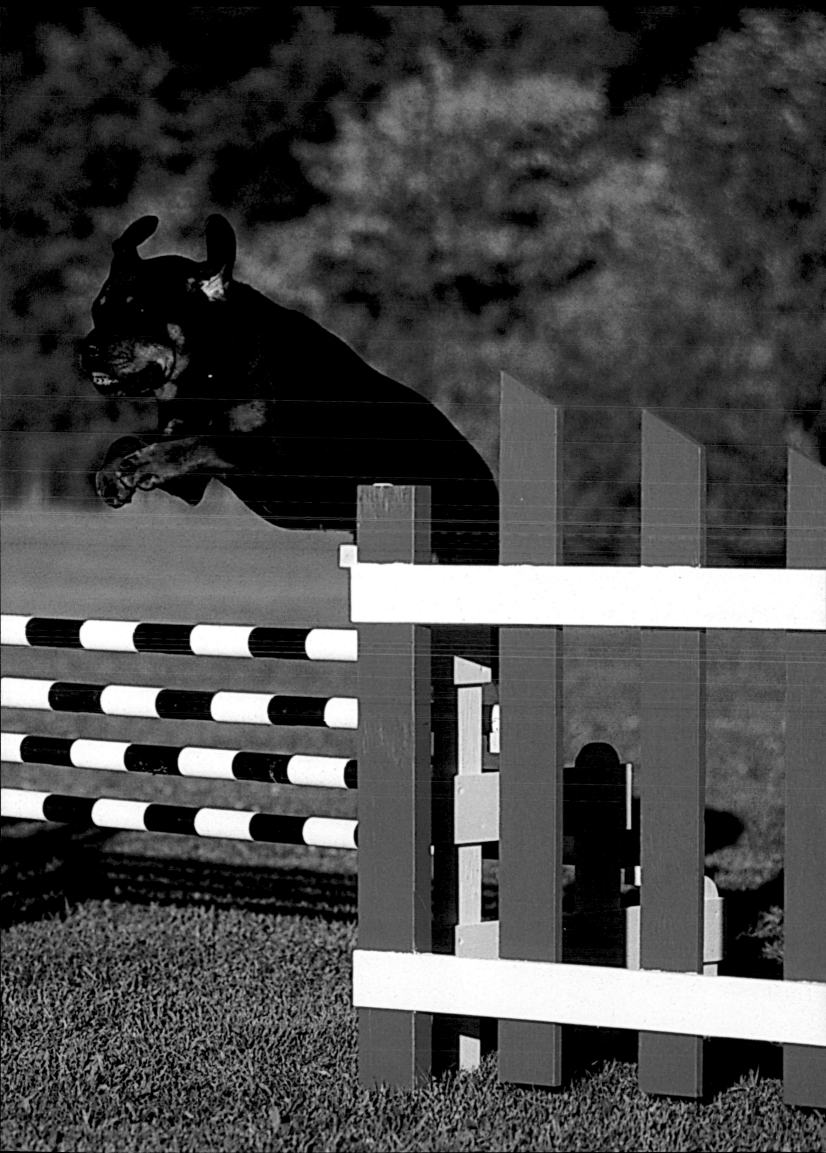

repackaging them as premium *Rottweilers*, he failed. He had the ingredients for good product but no niche. Before passing into cynological oblivion, however, Kull may have set in motion two effects that outlived his memory. First, crossing experiments by Kull with Leonbergers and traditional Rottweilers at the end of the nineteenth century may have produced the stock for the new-style Rottweiler developed by Graf and depicted in Strebel's illustration at the beginning of the twentieth century. All the characteristics that distinguish the Graf/Strebel Rottweiler from the traditional herding-dog Rottweiler — squarish croup, deep chest, deep muzzle, thick vertical forelegs — are to found in the *Sennenhund* (Alpine Dog) breeds in general and in the Leonberger in particular. Noteworthy in this connection is the high frequency of long coat and anomalous color that bedeviled both the DRK and IRK breed lines throughout their first decade.

Secondly, Kull's inventive marketing approach to the *Rottweiler* may have twigged better-connected breeders in the Neckar Valley such as Albert Graf to a more timely opportunity for the dog and its name. In the same year (1901) that IKLRH adopted its Standard, official interest was first expressed in using dogs for police work. Such a dog as might have been found in Kull's stock, possessed of the working skills and agility of a herding dog but more intimidating in build, would have seemed made-to-order for the new work of apprehending urban criminals and controlling urban crowds. Moreover, Rottweil, for six centuries the regional seat for the administration of imperial law in southwest Germany, would lend its draconian name very aptly to a *Polizeihund*. There was even a second semantically appropriate

resonance in the name: as well as "dog pack," *Rotte* means "patrol squad."

Whether Graf took his foundation dogs for the new-style Rottweiler from Kull's stock or elsewhere, the challenge of organizing the breed and marketing it for police work was all his. Graf certainly got off on the right foot in 1905, getting high-profile exposure at the Heidelberg Show and excellent copy from Strebel: the martial Ur-dog marching shoulder to shoulder with grim legions over the Saint Gothard Pass was a brilliant touch. For his enterprise, Graf had nearby both a model and a rival in the person of Captain Max von Stephanitz. In 1899, this iron-willed cavalry officer had founded the *Verein für Deutsche Schäferhunde* (SV, Association for German Shepherd Dogs) in Stuttgart, fifty miles up the Neckar from Heidelberg. SV, which remains the national breed society for the German Shepherd Dog to this day, was conceived as a breeding vehicle for Von Stephanitz' own dog, **Horand von Grafrath** 1 SZ. Horand was the first dog registered in the SV breed book and the sole foundation sire of the breed, from whom every purebred German Shepherd Dog in the world today is descended. Beginning in 1901, Von Stephanitz vigorously and effectively lobbied for the use of the German Shepherd Dog in police work, ensuring that it would dominate the field from the beginning.

The *Zeitgeist* of Imperial Germany at the turn of the century as personified by the militarist Von Turpitz and the eugenist Alfred Ploetz was highly receptive to the notion of putting trained highbred dogs in the uniformed ranks of the State, in part as an precursory analogy to what might be done with men. The Imperial German Army put German Shepherd Dogs to extensive use in trench warfare

during the Great War. During the Second World War, most of the best Rottweiler breedstock of the ADRK (renamed the *Fachschaft für Rottweiler* section of the *Reichsverband für Hundewesen*, for the nonce), being also the best-trained, was recruited by the Wehrmacht and lost in action.

Graf sought to duplicate Von Stephanitz' formula for setting up a successful police-dog breed, substituting his **Russ vom Brückenbuckel 1 DRZ** in place of Horand and his DRK in place of SV. Graf, however, immediately ran into problems. Lacking the political power and disciplinarian steel of President Von Stephanitz, Secretary Graf failed to enforce the coronation of Russ as sole foundation sire. The disaffected membership that

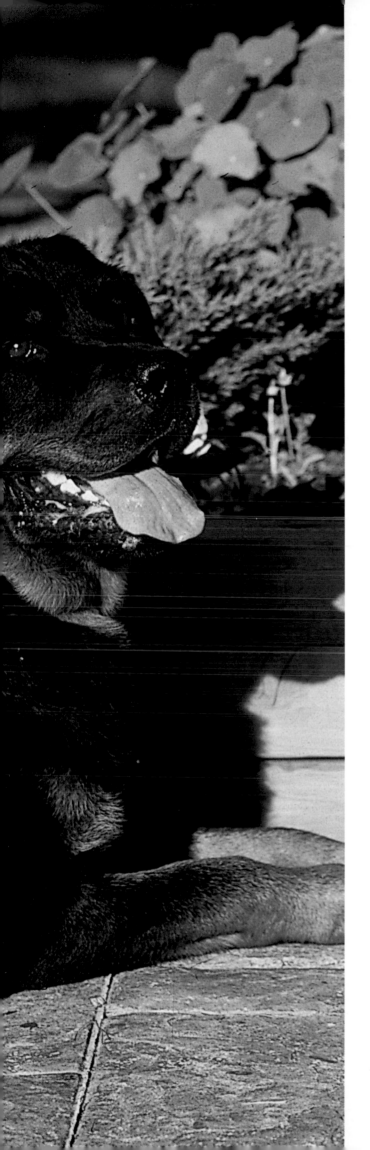

split from DRK soon rallied around the very different standard of **Leo von Cannstatt** 29 IRZ. In the light of subsequent developments, the nature of the "gross infringement" that precipitated the DRK split can be surmised: namely, an attempt to introduce mastiff-like elements from some other breed into the line out of Russ.

The IRK faction regarded the Graf/DRK Rottweiler as insufficiently differentiated in build and aptitude from the German Shepherd Dog, as both were descended from common herding-dog types. The earlier crossing with one of the Sennenhund breeds, which were also descended from herding-dog types, had not altered the DRK Rottweiler enough to offset the competitive advantage of the breed already dominant in police work. The perceived need to differentiate the Rottweiler by enhancing its mastiff-like features motivated the IRK breeding program. Picking up on a suggestion made by Dr Manfred Schanzle in 1967, Larry Elsden — former chairman of the Rottweiler Club in the UK — has recently proposed that the Boxer breed may have been crossed into the Rottweiler at this time.

The Boxer Klub was established in Munich in 1895. The original Munich strain Flocki, born 1895 — son of an old-style English Bulldog imported to Munich from England and grandson of a Brabanter Bullenbeisser imported to Munich from France. This original Boxer strain was much stockier and lower to the ground than today's Boxer. The stretching influence of Great Dane was not folded into the early Boxer line until shortly before the Great War. In photographs, the original stocky Boxers of Munich bear a striking resemblance to the first IRK Rottweilers that suddenly appeared in nearby Heidelberg in 1907.

In summary, the story that most satisfactorily explains the two abrupt physical transformations between 1882 and 1908 in the *Rottweiler* is that there were two corresponding episodes of cross-breeding. The first cross, at the end of the nineteenth century, was between the traditional Rottweiler herding-dog type and a heavier breed displaying Sennenhund-like qualities in the head and chest — the case has been made above for considering the Leonberger. This first cross-breed was, in the middle of the first decade of the twentieth century, then crossed again with a compact mastiff-like breed — perhaps the Boxer. The first cross yielded the DRK Rottweiler, which petered out in the 1920's. The second cross yielded the IRK/ADRK Rottweiler, which prevails worldwide today.